JAN 0 2 2016

DATE DUE

MAR 1 7 2001	JAN 2 5 2002	JUL 1 0 2013
NOV 1 9 2001		FEB 1 8 2014
JAN 2 2 2002	APR 2 1 2003	FEB 2 8 2015
MAR 1 9 2002	JAN 0 7 2004	SEP 0 7 2016
JUN 1 8 2002	OCT 2 7 2004	
AUG 1 6 2002	JUN 2 8 2005	
JAN 0 6 2003	APR 1 7 2007	
FEB 2 8 2004	JUN 07 2008	
	MAY 0 6 2009	
	NOV 0 7 2009	
	MAR 2 2 2010	
MAR 1 9 2011		

NEPTUNE

A TRUE BOOK

by

Larry Dane Brimner

Children's Press®
A Division of Grolier Publishing

New York   London   Hong Kong   Sydney
Danbury, Connecticut

Neptune's largest
moon, Triton

Subject Consultant
Peter Goodwin
Science Department Chairman
Kent School, Kent, CT

Reading Consultant
Linda Cornwell
Learning Resource Consultant
Indiana Department
of Education

Author's Dedication:
For El Cajon's Bostonia
Elementary School

Visit Children's Press® on the
Internet at:
http://publishing.grolier.com

Library of Congress Cataloging-in-Publication Data

Brimner, Larry Dane.
    Neptune : a true book / by Larry Dane Brimner.
        p.   cm. — (A True book)
    Includes bibliographical references and index.
    Summary: Describes the eighth planet from the Sun, Neptune, and its orbit, rotation, gassy surface, rings, moons, and the visit by the *Voyager 2* probe.
        ISBN 0-516-21157-9 (lib. bdg.)   0-516-26496-6 (pbk.)
        1. Neptune (Planet)—Juvenile literature. [1. Neptune (Planet)] I. Title. II. Series.
QB691.B75 1999
523.48'1—dc21
                                                            98-22039
                                                            CIP
                                                            AC

GROLIER
PUBLISHING

Contents

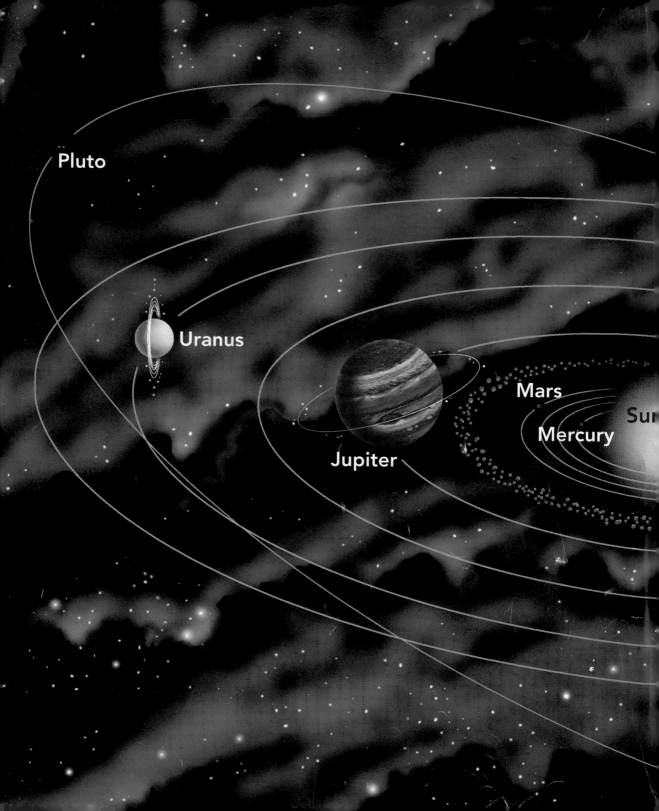

The Solar System

Venus

Earth   Moon

Asteroid Belt

Saturn

Neptune

Looking Beyond Saturn

Nine planets travel around the Sun in paths called "orbits." These planets, along with all the other objects orbiting the Sun, make up our solar system.

We haven't always known that nine planets make up

Neptune is one of nine planets in our solar system.

the solar system. Before early
sky watchers used telescopes,
they thought there were only
six planets. They believed
Saturn was the most distant
planet. Then, in 1781, William
Herschel (1738–1822) discovered a seventh planet,
Uranus, far beyond Saturn!
Were there others? Many
astronomers started looking
for more.

An Eighth Planet

Astronomers noticed that Uranus did not act like other planets. They could figure out the orbits of the other planets. But Uranus wasn't always where they thought it should be. This made some astronomers think that a "missing planet" was making Uranus behave oddly.

John C. Adams

In 1845, John C. Adams (1819–1892) used math to figure out where this missing planet should be. Unfortunately, the British astronomer and mathematician was young and unknown. So no one listened to him.

A French mathematician named Urbain J. J. Leverrier (1811–1877) had better luck. He came up with the same theory, or idea, as Adams, and sent it to Johann G. Galle (1812–1910) at the Urania Observatory in Berlin, Germany. Galle received it

Urbain J. J. Leverrier used mathematics to find Neptune.

Neptune was the Roman god of the sea.

on September 23, 1846. That night he found the solar system's eighth planet. It was right where Adams and Leverrier had said it would be! The planet was named Neptune, after the Roman god of the sea.

The Planet

Neptune is almost 2.8 billion miles (4.5 billion kilometers) from the Sun. This is more than 30 times farther from the Sun than our planet Earth. The time it takes for a planet to orbit once around the Sun is the length of its year. Earth takes 365 days,

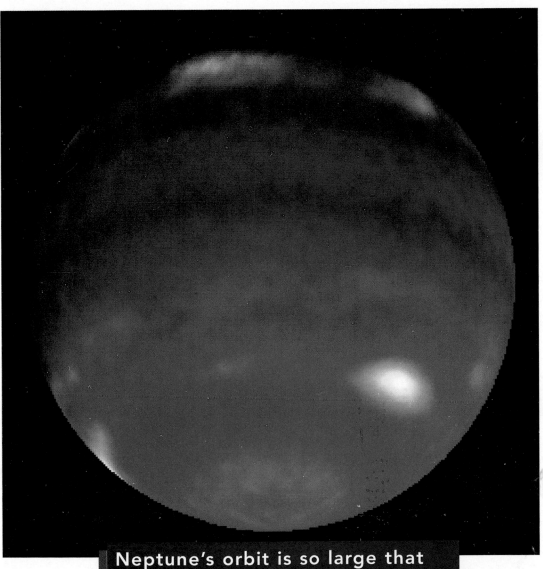

Neptune's orbit is so large that the planet hasn't even completed one orbit since it was discovered.

or one year, to make its journey. But Neptune is so far away from the Sun that it takes 165 Earth-years to make one orbit. One "year" on Neptune is 165 Earth-years long! The planet has not completed even one orbit since it was discovered in 1846.

A planet rotates, or spins, on its axis as it journeys around the Sun. An axis is an imaginary line that runs between a planet's north and

Which Planet Is Farthest?

Usually Pluto is the farthest planet from the Sun. Sometimes, though, Pluto's orbit takes it inside Neptune's orbit. When this happens, Neptune is the most distant planet in the solar system.

The planet Pluto

south poles. It's rotation brings daylight to the side of the planet facing the Sun and nighttime to the side in darkness. It takes Earth 24 hours to make one complete rotation. This is the length of one full day on Earth. Neptune rotates a little faster. Its day is only about 16 hours long.

Neptune is one of the planets known as the "gas giants." The others are Jupiter, Saturn, and Uranus.

Neptune's rotation
causes its day and
night.

The gas giants are very different from Earth. Earth is a rocky planet. You can walk and play on its surface because it is solid. The gas giants have no solid surface.

Neptune is the fourth-largest planet in the solar system. Jupiter, Saturn, and Uranus are larger. Neptune is 30,775 miles (50,000 km) across the middle. That's almost four times wider than our own Earth!

Jupiter (top), Saturn (above), and Uranus (right) are the other gas giants.

People could not survive on Neptune because it doesn't have oxygen—the gas we need to live. Also, Neptune is a very cold planet. Temperatures there dip to –360 degrees Fahrenheit (–218 degrees Celsius). Scientists do not believe there is any life on this distant planet.

Neptune is a windy place, just like the other gas giants. Winds howl across the planet at speeds up to 1,490 miles

Very strong winds push clouds across Neptune.

Neptune's Rings

For a long time, scientists thought Neptune might have rings. But Neptune was so far away that they couldn't see it clearly through their telescopes on Earth. Then in 1977, the National Aeronautics and Space Administration (NASA) launched a probe, or space-

Even through a telescope, Neptune cannot be seen clearly from Earth.

craft, called *Voyager 2*, into space. *Voyager 2* was like a flying science laboratory with equipment and cameras to study the planets it flew by. At first, the probe was only supposed to go as far as Jupiter and Saturn. But *Voyager 2* did such a good job that the scientists on Earth sent it on to Uranus and Neptune.

Voyager 2 flew by Neptune in 1989 after a twelve-year journey. From June until October, its equipment studied the planet and took photographs. We learned more about Neptune in those few months

Voyager 2 flew by Neptune in 1989 and gave us a close-up view of the planet and its moons.

than we had known since the planet was discovered. One important discovery was that Neptune has rings. This was exciting news. It meant that all the gas giants have rings.

Neptune has four rings that scientists have named, and there may be another. Scientists aren't sure of the exact number because Neptune's rings are thin and hard to see. They are not colorful like Saturn's. They are made up of countless particles, or pieces, of dark space dust. In some parts, the rings look brighter and thicker.

Neptune's rings are very thin and made of space dust.

Scientists think the dust particles have clumped together in these areas. They are not sure why this happens.

Where's the Spot?

Voyager 2 photographed some amazing sites on Neptune. One surprising sight was the Great Dark Spot. Scientists think it was a fierce storm about the size of our planet Earth. Some of the most powerful winds in the solar system were measured there.

In June 1994, the Hubble Space Telescope—a giant telescope orbiting in space—tried to find the Great Dark Spot again. It was missing! Did the storm end? Was it covered by clouds? Scientists aren't certain yet. But they have found another storm spot that wasn't there before.

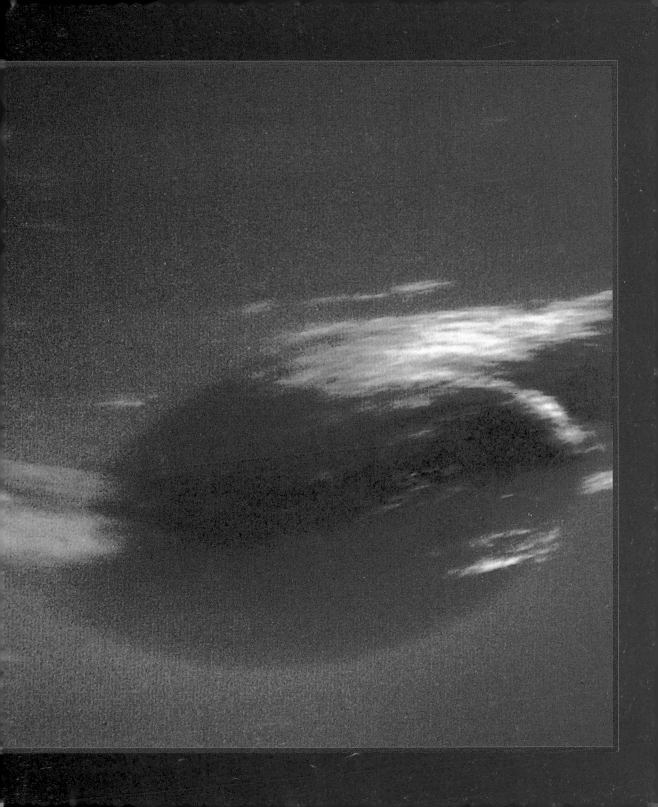

Neptune's Moons

For many years, scientists thought Neptune had only two moons. Then British astronomer named William Lassell (1799–1880) made an important discovery. He spotted Neptune's large moon, Triton, only about a month after the planet itself

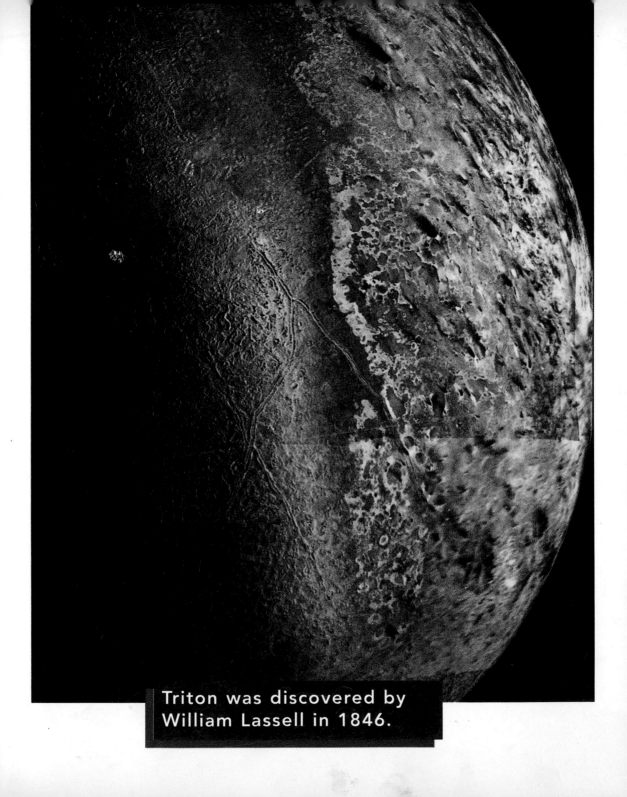

Triton was discovered by
William Lassell in 1846.

was discovered. Then in 1949, a smaller moon named Nereid was discovered.

Voyager 2 found six more moons orbiting the planet. Today we know that at least eight moons orbit Neptune. Seven are small and one is large. There may even be others that scientists have not yet discovered.

Triton is Neptune's largest moon. It is slightly smaller than Earth's Moon.

Smaller moons, such as this one above, also orbit Neptune.

Triton is very unique because it has a backward orbit. This means that Triton orbits Neptune in a direction that is opposite to Neptune's rotation. It is the only large moon in the solar system known to do this.

Scientists think Triton may be the coldest place in the solar system. It is a frozen chunk of ice and rock. Temperatures on its surface get as low as −391°F (−235°C).

Voyager 2 also found that Triton's surface is covered by large cracks. Photographs from the probe show frozen nitrogen gas and dark dust exploding from those cracks. Scientists think the frozen gas and dust fall back to Triton's surface. This may give Triton its unusual streaky appearance.

Neptune and its icy moon Triton seem like places you could find only in movies. Yet we know they exist in our solar system. Perhaps one day they will give us clues to how the solar system began.

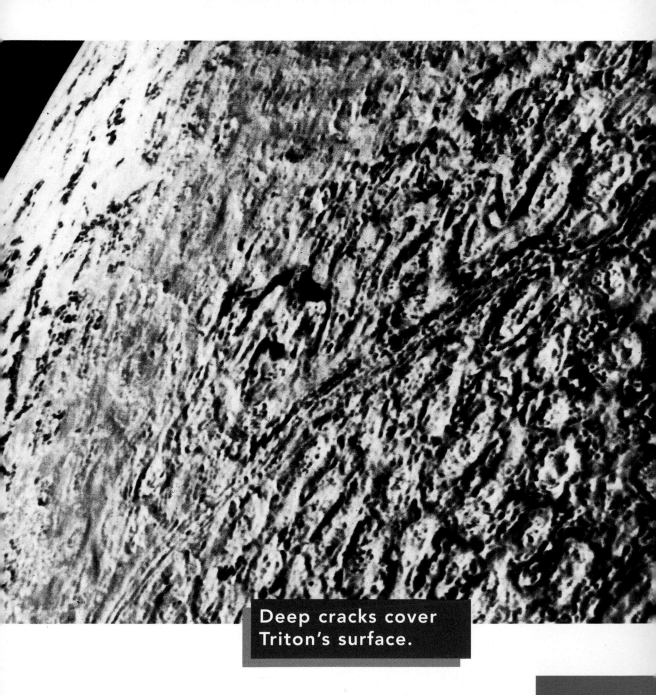

Deep cracks cover
Triton's surface.

Neptune Quick Facts

Diameter	30,775 miles (50,000 km)
Average distance from the Sun	2.8 billion miles (4.5 billion km)
Average temperature (atmosphere)	−360°F (−218°C)
Length of day	16 hours 7 minutes
Length of year	165 Earth-years
Moons	8 (known)

Mission to Neptune

Mission	Launch Date
Voyager 2	August 20, 1977 (reached Neptune on August 24, 1989)

To Find Out More

Here are more places to learn about Neptune and other planets in space:

 **Books**

Bailey, Donna. **The Far Planets.** Steck-Vaughn Company, 1991.

Branley, Franklyn M. **Neptune: Voyager's Final Target.** HarperCollins, 1992.

Brewer, Duncan. **The Outer Planets: Uranus, Neptune, Pluto.** Marshall Cavendish, 1993.

Landau, Elaine. **Neptune.** Franklin Watts, 1991.

Organizations and Online Sites

The Children's Museum of Indianapolis
3000 N. Meridian Street
Indianapolis, IN 46208
(317) 924-5431
http://childrensmuseum.org/sq1.htm

Visit the SpaceQuest Planetarium to see what it has to offer, including a view of this month's night sky.

National Aeronautics and Space Administration (NASA)
http://www.nasa.gov

At NASA's home page, you can access information about its exciting history and present resources and missions.

National Air and Space Museum
Smithsonian Institution
601 Independence Ave. SW
Washington, DC 20560
(202) 357-1300
http://www.nasm.si.edu/

The National Air and Space Museum site gives you up-to-date information about its programs and exhibits.

The Nine Planets
http://seds.lpl.arizona.edu/nineplanets/nineplanets/

Take a multimedia tour of the solar system and all its planets and moons.

Space Telescope Science Institute
3700 San Martin Drive
Johns Hopkins University
Homewood Campus
Baltimore, MD 21218
(410) 338-4700
http://www.stsci.edu//

The Space Telescope Science Institute operates the Hubble Space Telescope. Visit this site to see pictures of the telescope's outer-space view.

Windows to the Universe
http://windows.engin.umich.edu/

This site lets you click on all nine planets to find information about each one. It also covers many other space subjects, including important historical figures, scientists, and astronauts.

Important Words

astronomer a scientist who studies objects in space

axis an imaginary line about which a planet turns

orbit to travel around an object

oxygen a gas people need to breathe

pole either end of a planet's axis

probe a spacecraft used to study space

rotate to spin

solar system a group of planets and other objects that orbit around a star, such as our Sun

telescope an instrument that makes faraway objects look closer

theory an idea

Index

Meet the Author

Larry Dane Brimner taught school for twenty years and now writes full time for children. When he isn't writing, he enjoys riding his mountain bike in the San Juan Mountains around Rico, Colorado, and adding to his collections of stars, whirligigs, and birdhouses. He is the author of many award-winning books, including *Merry Christmas, Old Armadillo* (Boyds Mills Press). His recent titles for Children's Press include *Dinosaurs Dance* and *Bobsledding and the Luge.*